MW01234904

DESTINY
Journal

Recording Your Path to a Life of Divine Order

T. D. Jakes

Faith
Words

New York   Boston   Nashville

FaithWords
Hachette Book Group
1290 Avenue of the Americas
New York, NY 10104

www.faithwords.com

Printed in the United States of America

RRD-C

First Edition: January 2016
10 9 8 7 6 5 4 3 2 1

FaithWords is a division of Hachette Book Group, Inc.
The FaithWords name and logo are trademarks of Hachette Book Group, Inc.

The Hachette Speakers Bureau provides a wide range of authors for speaking events. To find out more, go to www.hachettespeakersbureau.com or call (866) 376-6591.

The publisher is not responsible for websites (or their content) that are not owned by the publisher.

ISBN 978-1-4555-5396-9 (hardcover)

If I am wise I will see the predestined purpose
I was created for and, in my brief life span,
find it and do it.

....
....
....
....
....
....
....
....
....
....
....
....
....
....
....
....
....
....
....

....
....
....
....
....
....
....
....
....
....
....
....
....
....
....
....
....
....
....
....
....
....

*I was created to fulfill some role only through
which I can find the great elixir of contentment
and courage.*

When I watch people fully engaged in their purpose, it's confirmation that God has given each of us a destiny.

....
....
....
....
....
....
....
....
....
....
....
....
....
....
....
....
....
....

I can't define success in dollars or cents.
It can only be quantified by the
accomplishment of a predestined purpose!

Destiny is the push of my instinct to the pull of my purpose.

....
....
....
....
....
....
....
....
....
....
....
....
....
....
....
....
....
....
....
....

What gravity is to the order of our
universe, Destiny is to the meaning of life.

Destiny pulls me beyond the familiar toward my future.

When instinct and purpose connect, their progeny is Destiny.

*My peace and power come from digging
beneath the surface and locating my own core
of potential.*

....
....
....
....
....
....
....
....
....
....
....
....
....
....
....
....
....
....
....
....
....

Destiny is so much bigger than I am. I will trust that the results are not in my hands.

I will find the destiny my Creator has designed for me.

*Destiny gently pulls me through wandering
mediocrity.*

All I have been exposed to and all that I have experienced are in the repository that builds my future.

....

....

....

....

....

....

....

....

....

....

....

....

....

....

....

....

....

....

....
....
....
....
....
....
....
....
....
....
....
....
....
....
....
....
....

God's purpose for my life cannot manifest in the
midst of chaos.

*The time to shift my priorities in the direction
of Destiny is never convenient.*

....
....
....
....
....
....
....
....
....
....
....
....
....
....
....
....
....
....

....
....
....
....
....
....
....
....
....
....
....
....
....
....
....
....
....
....
....
....
....
....

The first thing to do in deciding what stays in my life and what goes is to determine what nourishes me and strengthens me.

I will share my dream only with people who want me to succeed.

....
....
....
....
....
....
....
....
....
....
....
....
....
....
....
....
....
....

Even if no one else can see what's inside me, I do.

I value myself. Imagine the world without me. I realize I am priceless.

....

....

....

....

....

....

....

....

....

....

....

....

....

....

....

....

....

....

....

....

I will set my priorities for Destiny and forget about what other people want for me, no matter how well meaning their intentions.

Only I can have the vision for my life, so only I can determine what's most important to getting there.

....
....
....
....
....
....
....
....
....
....
....
....
....
....
....
....
....
....
....

....

....

....

....

....

....

....

....

....

....

....

....

....

....

....

....

....

....

People who are living life on purpose have
priorities and tend to get more out of life.

Greatness runs deep, but pettiness runs shallow and wide.

_I will stop allowing minor thoughts to occupy my
mind; they're not paying rent to reside there!_

The pain I have been through, the losses, the humiliation, and the betrayal are all stepping-stones to a higher place in Destiny.

....
....
....
....
....
....
....
....
....
....
....
....
....
....
....
....
....
....

....

....

....

....

....

....

....

....

....

....

....

....

....

....

....

....

....

....

*I reserve my strength for the difficult matters of
arriving at Destiny.*

Order is essential, but life is full of changes.
Sometimes life does not always fit
a certain order.

....
....
....
....
....
....
....
....
....
....
....
....
....
....
....
....
....
....
....
....
....
....

God can use disorder to create a new order
in my life.

*Nobody likes to lose, but that doesn't mean
every conflict or struggle I encounter in life is
worth a fight.*

....
....
....
....
....
....
....
....
....
....
....
....
....
....
....
....
....
....

....

....

....

....

....

....

....

....

....

....

....

....

....

....

....

....

....

....

Working toward my destiny is a daily endeavor.

Destiny is a long-distance race where endurance is the key to winning.

*Destiny belongs to those who demand it by their
faithful and dogged determination to hang in
there until they achieve what they desire.*

*Destiny is the ultimate expression of fully
being myself, making my own choices.*

....
....
....
....
....
....
....
....
....
....
....
....
....
....
....
....
....
....
....
....
....

It is in the pursuit of Destiny that I discover
what a fascinating person I am.

Some overcome incredible odds and pass through hell and high water to meet up with Destiny.

....
....
....
....
....
....
....
....
....
....
....
....
....
....
....
....
....
....

I can't deny where I came from, but I can learn from it, grow from it, and build upon it to go higher.

Destiny cannot be tricked by cheap imitations.

....
....
....
....
....
....
....
....
....
....
....
....
....
....
....
....
....

If I don't invest in myself, no one else will, either.

*Pursuing Destiny is not for wimps. I can't
back down or cower away.*

....

....

....

....

....

....

....

....

....

....

....

....

....

....

....

....

....

....

....

....

*Understanding that I have been chosen to play
the lead role in my life is a critical Destiny step.*

This is my life. No rehearsals. No retakes.
No delete button.

No one can take my place to fulfill my destiny.

Destiny has no expiration date!

....
....
....
....
....
....
....
....
....
....
....
....
....
....
....
....
....
....

*Life has all types of disturbances that I must
struggle to overcome.*

My toughest storms are those that other people can't see.

....
....
....
....
....
....
....
....
....
....
....
....
....
....
....
....
....
....

....
....
....
....
....
....
....
....
....
....
....
....
....
....
....
....
....
....
....
....
....
....
....

No one can see clearly in a storm. That's why I must walk by faith and not simply by what I can see.

God has plans for me even in the storm. Just because I am in a storm does not negate the presence of God.

....

....

....

....

....

....

....

....

....

....

....

....

....

....

....

....

....

....

....

God has reserved a place for me in life that is my destiny.

I commit myself to find out where I belong
and determine how to get there.

....
....
....
....
....
....
....
....
....
....
....
....
....
....
....
....
....
....
....
....

I am wise enough to know that, right now,
I am smart enough, attractive enough, and
secure enough to walk the trail of Destiny.

Living through others is not my Destiny.

....

....

....

....

....

....

....

....

....

....

....

....

....

....

....

....

....

....

....

....

....

Sometimes my challenges and difficulties are
what cause me to know the value of what I
have accomplished.

Destiny cannot and will not be rushed.

....

....

....

....

....

....

....

....

....

....

....

....

....

....

....

....

....

There is a plan for my life.

*I will not to be so consumed with reaching my
destiny that I ignore that Destiny is a process.*

....
....
....
....
....
....
....
....
....
....
....
....
....
....
....
....
....
....
....
....
....
....

....

....

....

....

....

....

....

....

....

....

....

....

....

....

....

....

....

....

I will enjoy the times of my life, even the bumpy moments.

Looking at the clock to judge my accomplishments can make me want to give up. I will always keep pushing.

....
....
....
....
....
....
....
....
....
....
....
....
....
....
....
....
....
....
....

....
....
....
....
....
....
....
....
....
....
....
....
....
....
....
....
....
....
....
....
....

*I will get out and live the life God has intended
for me. Only I can live it.*

I won't leave my God-given gifts unopened.

....
....
....
....
....
....
....
....
....
....
....
....
....
....
....
....
....
....
....
....
....

....
....
....
....
....
....
....
....
....
....
....
....
....
....
....
....
....
....
....
....
....
....
....

*I will rip off the lid of my abilities, tear into that
box that is my talents, and use every gift God
has given me.*

I devote myself to fulfilling the unique purpose that is my destiny.

....
....
....
....
....
....
....
....
....
....
....
....
....
....
....
....
....
....
....

*I won't spend my time obsessing about what
others are doing. Traveling my own path to
Destiny is all-consuming.*

When I make it through, I learn that God is able to send me people and resources that I never imagined.

....
....
....
....
....
....
....
....
....
....
....
....
....
....
....
....
....
....
....

....

....

....

....

....

....

....

....

....

....

....

....

....

....

....

....

....

....

....

....

....

Each experience, each challenge, each lesson will take me to the next dimension, building on what's already inside me.

What matters most is not found in the destination but is revealed in the issues that I have to resolve along the way to Destiny.

....
....
....
....
....
....
....
....
....
....
....
....
....
....
....
....
....
....
....
....

*I will look deeper at my life and the uniqueness
of its complications for clues that unfold Destiny.*

Every strange, dysfunctional, or unexplainable event in my life helped make me the person I am.

....

....

....

....

....

....

....

....

....

....

....

....

....

....

....

....

....

....

*Destiny is for the daring and determined who
are willing to endure some discomfort, delay
gratification, and go where Destiny leads.*

To wake up every day with an agenda is to have a purpose!

....
....
....
....
....
....
....
....
....
....
....
....
....
....
....
....
....
....
....
....

....
....
....
....
....
....
....
....
....
....
....
....
....
....
....
....
....
....
....
....
....

The complexity of Destiny means accepting the
difficult side of my purpose in life.

As I follow my instinct to connect to my purpose, I understand that challenges pave the way to Destiny.

....

....

....

....

....

....

....

....

....

....

....

....

....

....

....

....

....

....

....

....

....

....

*I'm most tempted to give up when I'm in the
midst of trouble. I will remind myself that
challenge is part of my destiny.*

I won't limit my thinking with tunnel vision.

When Destiny is calling, I may get kicked out of the small place where I am, to be received into a larger place.

I will stay faithful to Destiny each step of the way. I don't know which day will be that *day.*

....
....
....
....
....
....
....
....
....
....
....
....
....
....
....
....
....
....
....
....

....
....
....
....
....
....
....
....
....
....
....
....
....
....
....
....
....
....
....

One phone call, one meeting, one random
encounter can change my life.

I am closer to Destiny than ever, wiser than I have ever been, because I've learned from the ups and downs I have experienced.

....
....
....
....
....
....
....
....
....
....
....
....
....
....
....
....
....
....

....

....

....

....

....

....

....

....

....

....

....

....

....

....

....

....

....

....

Destiny is both a promise and a process.

I will let God fight the battles I can't win
by myself.

*Destiny requires a commitment to
lifelong learning.*

Destiny is a journey made of a series of stops rather than a single destination.

....
....
....
....
....
....
....
....
....
....
....
....
....
....
....
....
....
....
....

Going where Destiny calls means trying again
after failure.

Failure does not have to be the end of my dance with Destiny. It can become what gets me back out on the floor again.

....
....
....
....
....
....
....
....
....
....
....
....
....
....
....
....
....
....
....
....

I won't let fear block God's destiny for me.

*Destiny's knowledge comes to those who are
properly positioned to learn.*

....
....
....
....
....
....
....
....
....
....
....
....
....
....
....
....
....
....
....
....
....

I will allow my curious mind to wander into
new places Destiny opens to me.

Next to the voice of God, my own voice is the most important one I will hear.

....
....
....
....
....
....
....
....
....
....
....
....
....
....
....
....
....
....
....
....
....
....
....

．

Destiny constantly gives me opportunities for
exposure to the new, different, and greater.

I will corral my fears and move ahead with courage, daring to be the human marvel God created me to be.

....
....
....
....
....
....
....
....
....
....
....
....
....
....
....
....
....
....

....

....

....

....

....

....

....

....

....

....

....

....

....

....

....

....

....

....

My decisions will lead me to my destiny. Putting
great decisions in motion will change my life.

I rest in the assurance that God is with me.

I find fulfillment in the life Destiny has drawn me into.

It takes courage to make Destiny decisions.

....
....
....
....
....
....
....
....
....
....
....
....
....
....
....
....
....
....
....
....

God has provided and prepared everything I need. I need only take a step toward it.

Destiny is calling out to me.

*I am ready, ready, ready to elevate my mind to
the high calling of Destiny.*